ALMOST PERSUADED

Words and Music by
GLENN SUTTON and BILLY SHERRILL

Moderately slow waltz ♩ = 92

6

ANYTIME

Words and Music by
HAPPY LAWSON

Anytime - 2 - 1

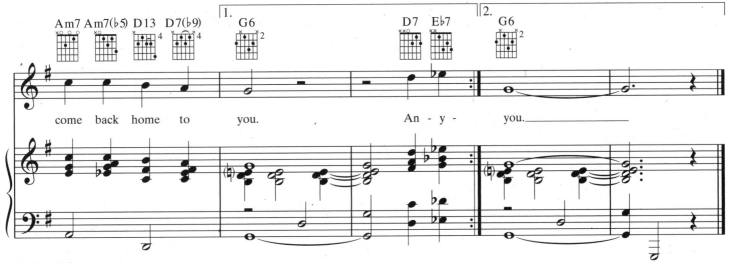

BOUQUET OF ROSES

Words and Music by
STEVE NELSON and BOB HILLIARD

Bouquet of Roses - 3 - 1

DON'T WORRY

Words and Music by
MARTY ROBBINS

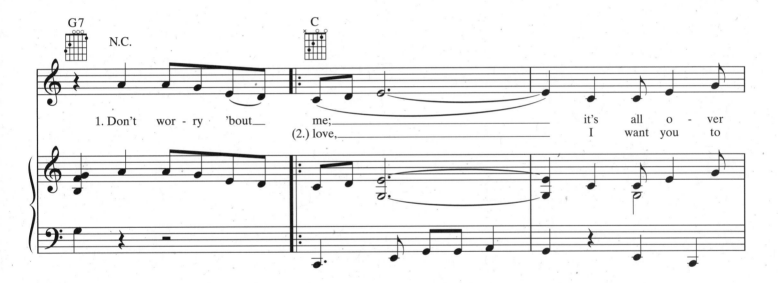

1. Don't wor-ry 'bout me; it's all o-ver
(2.) love, I want you to

now. Though I may be blue, I'll man-age some-
be as hap-py as I when you loved

DON'T TAKE YOUR GUNS TO TOWN

Words and Music by
JOHNNY CASH

young cow - boy named Bil - ly Joe___ grew rest - less on the farm,___ a

boy filled___ with wan - der - lust___ who real - ly meant no harm. He

changed his clothes and shined his boots and combed his dark hair down, and his

mother cried as he walked out:__ "Don't take your guns to town, son.

Leave your guns__ at home, Bill. Don't take your guns to

Moderately ♩ = 96

town." 2. He

Verses 2–5:

laughed and kissed his mom and said, "Your__ Bil - ly Joe's a man. He__
(3.) sang a song as on he rode, his__ guns hung at his hips. and__
(4.) drank his first strong li - quor then to__ calm his shak - ing hand, but the
5. Bill was raged and Bil - ly Joe reached__ for his gun to draw,

Freely

take your guns_ to town, son. Leave your guns_ at home, Bill. Don't take your guns to

1.–4.

Moderately ♩ = 96 (Tempo I)

town."

3. He
4. He

5.

town."

dim. poco a poco

EL PASO

Words and Music by
MARTY ROBBINS

Bright country waltz ♩. = 69

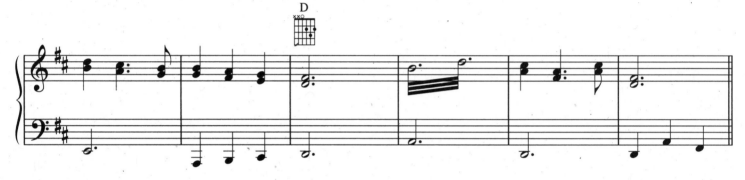

Verse 1:

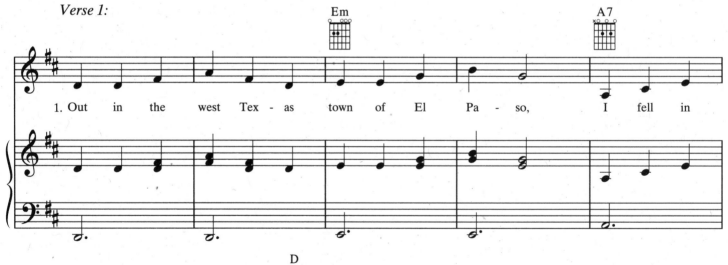

1. Out in the west Tex - as town of El Pa - so, I fell in

love with a Mex - i - can girl._____

El Paso - 8 - 1

wrong, for I feel a deep burn-ing pain in my side._____

Though I am try-ing to stay in the sad-dle, I'm get-ting wea-ry, un-

a-ble to ride. 8. But my love for____ Fe-

26

Verse 8:

li - na is strong and I rise where I've fall - en. Though I am

wea - ry, I can't stop to rest._____

I see the white puff of smoke from the ri - fle. I feel the bul - let go

deep in my chest._____

THE END OF THE WORLD

Words and Music by
ARTHUR KENT and SYLVIA DEE

Slowly ♩. = 72

Verses 1 & 2:

1. Why_____ does the sun_____ go on shin - ing?_____
2. Why_____ do the birds_____ go on sing - ing?_____

Why_____ does the sea rush to shore?_____
Why_____ do the stars glow a - bove?_____

The End of the World - 5 - 1

30

ev - 'ry - thing's_ the same_____ as it was._____ I
can't un - der - stand, no, I can't un - der - stand how
life goes on the way it does.

Verse 3:

3. Why_____ does my heart go on beat - ing?_____

The End of the World - 5 - 5

FLOWERS ON THE WALL

Words and Music by
LEW DEWITT

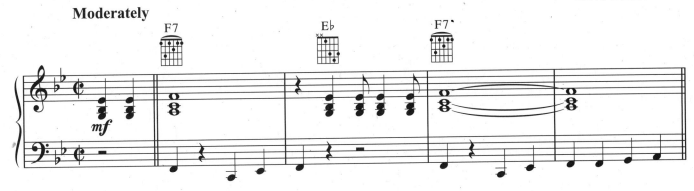

Verse:

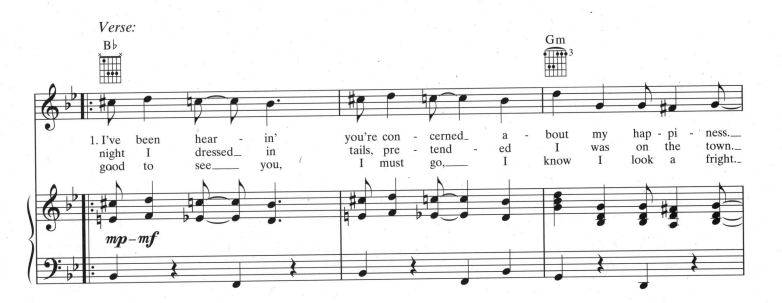

1. I've been hear-in' you're con-cerned a-bout my hap-pi-ness.
night I dressed in tails, pre-tend-ed I was on the town.
good to see you, I must go, I know I look a fright.

But all that thought you're giv-in' me is
As long as I can dream it's hard to
An-y way, my eyes are not ac-

Flowers on the Wall - 3 - 1

FADED LOVE

Moderate country two-beat

Words and Music by
BOB WILLS and JOHNNIE LEE WILLS

1.3.5.6.(etc.)

(Repeat ad lib. and fade) 2.4.

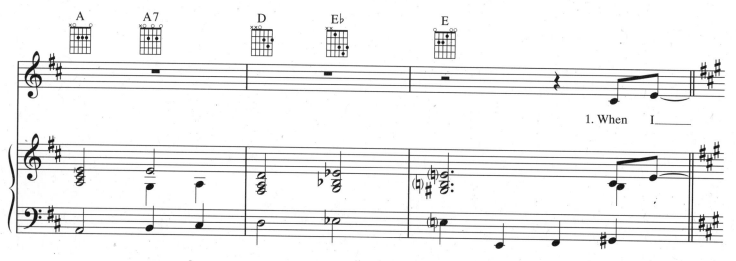

1. When I____

Faded Love - 4 - 1

Chorus:

I miss you, dar-lin', more and more__ ev-'ry day,__

__ as heav-en would miss the stars__ a-bove.__

With ev-'ry heart-beat I still think of you,__

__ and re-mem-ber our fad-ed love.__

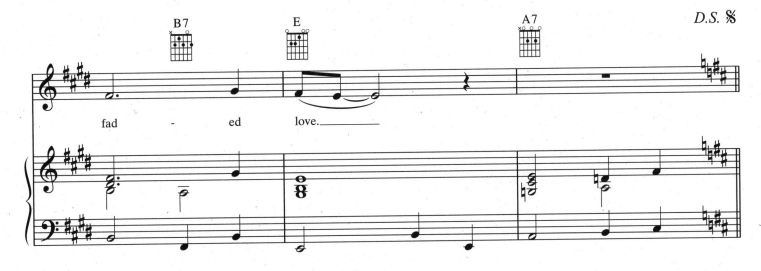

FIVE FEET HIGH AND RISING

Words and Music by
JOHNNY CASH

Moderately ♩ = 80

1. How high is the wa-ter, Ma-ma? Two feet high and
2. How high is the wa-ter, Ma-ma? Three feet high and
3. How high in the wa-ter, Ma-ma? Four feet high and
4. How high is the wa-ter, Ma-ma? Five feet high and

ris-ing. How high is the wa-ter, Pa-pa? She said it's
ris-ing. How high is the wa-ter, Pa-pa? She said it's
ris-ing. How high is the wa-ter, Pa-pa? She said it's
ris-ing. How high is the wa-ter, Pa-pa? She said it's

two feet high and ris-ing. But can we make it to the road in a
three feet high and ris-ing. Well, the hives are gone; I
four feet high and ris-ing. Hey, come look through the
five feet high and ris-ing. Well, the rails are washed out

Five Feet High and Rising - 2 - 1

FOUR WALLS

Words and Music by
MARVIN J. MOORE and GEORGE H. CAMPBELL, JR.

Slowly, with feeling

Verse:

1. Out where the bright lights are glow-ing_____ you're
2.3. *See additional lyrics*

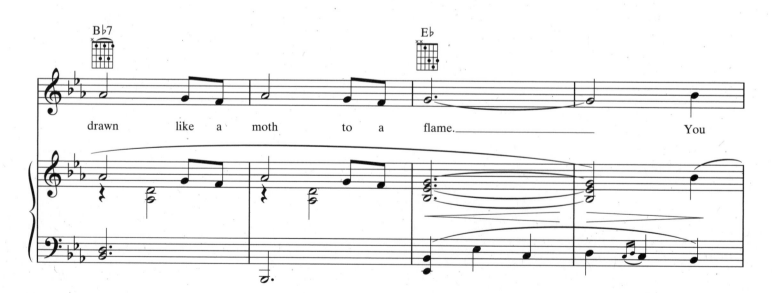

drawn like a moth to a flame._____ You

Four Walls - 3 - 1

laugh while the wine's o - ver - flow - ing, _____ while

I sit and whis - per your name. _____

Chorus:

Four walls to hear me, _____

four walls to _____ see, _____

four walls too near me,

clos - ing in on me!

me!

Verse 2:
Sometimes I ask why I'm waiting,
But my walls have nothing to say.
I'm made for love, not for hating.
So here, where you left me, I'll stay.
(To Chorus:)

Verse 3:
One night with you is like heaven.
And so while I'm walking the floor,
I'll listen for steps in the hallway
And wait for your knock on my door.
(To Chorus:)

THE HANGING TREE

Words by
MACK DAVID

Music by
JERRY LIVINGSTON

Moderately, with a steady rhythm ♩ = 96

HARPER VALLEY P.T.A.

Words and Music by
TOM T. HALL

Moderately (with a heavy beat)

I want to tell you all a story 'bout a Har-per Val-ley wid-owed wife__
note said, "Mis-sus John-son, you're wear-ing your dress-es way too
hap-pened that the P. T. A. was gon-na meet that ver-y af-ter-

high.
noon. It's re-port-ed you've been drink-ing and a-
They were sure sur-prised when Mis-sus John-son

who had a teen-age daugh-ter who at-

Harper Valley P.T.A. - 4 - 1

tend - ed Har - per Val - ley Jun - ior High.
run - nin' 'round with men and go - ing wild.
wore her min - i - skirt in - to the room.

Well, her
And we
And as she

D7

daugh - ter came home one af - ter - noon, and did - n't e - ven stop to play.
don't be - lieve you ought to be a - bring - ing up your lit - tle girl this way."
walked up to the black - board, I still re - call the words she had to say;

G7   A7

She said, "Mom, I got a note here from the
It was signed by the sec - re - tar - y,
she said, "I'd like to ad - dress this meet - ing

Har - per Val - ley P. T. A."
Har - per Val - ley P. T. A."
of the Har - per Val - ley P. T.

1. 2.

D7

A."   The
                                    Well, it

3.

B♭7

"Well, there's

Bob - by Tay - lor, sit - tin' there, and sev - en times he's asked me for a date;
Har - per could - n't be here 'cause he stayed too long at Kel - ly's Bar a - gain,

Mis - sus Tay - lor sure seems to use a lot of ice when - ev - er he's a -
and if you smell Shir - ley Thomp - son's breath, you'll find she's had a lit - tle nip of

way."
gin."

"And Mis - ter Bak - er, can you tell us why your
"Then you have the nerve to tell me you
would - n't put you on be - cause it

sec - re - tar - y had to leave this town,
think that as a moth - er I'm not fit.
real - ly did, it hap - pened just this way,

and should - n't
Well, this is
the day my

HIGH NOON
(Do Not Forsake Me)

Lyrics by
NED WASHINGTON

Music by
DIMITRI TIOMKIN

Moderately

Do not for-sake me, oh, my dar-lin'

on this, our wed-ding day.

Do not for - sake me, oh, my dar - lin'.

Wait,_____ wait a - long!_____

I do not know what fate a - waits me._____

I on - ly know I must be brave,_____

58

darlin'._____ You made that prom-ise as a

bride._____ Do not for-sake me, oh, my

darlin'._____ Al-tho' you're griev-in',

don't think of leav-in', now that I need you

High Noon - 6 - 5

I DON'T HURT ANYMORE

Words and Music by
JACK ROLLINS and DON ROBERTSON

Moderately slow, with a beat ♩ = 96

I don't hurt an-y-more; ___ all my tear-drops are dried. ___ No more walk-in' the floor ___ with that burn-ing in-side. ___ Just to think it could be,

I Don't Hurt Anymore - 3 - 1

I Don't Hurt Anymore - 3 - 3

I GOT STRIPES

Words and Music by
JOHNNY CASH and CHARLIE WILLIAMS

I'M MOVIN' ON

Words and Music by
HANK SNOW

I'll soon be gone.
Oh, hear my song.
Keep roll - in' on.
I'm roll - in' on.
You stayed a - way too long."

You were fly - in' too high for my lit - tle old sky, so I'm
You had the laugh on me, so I've set you free, and I'm
You're gon - na ease my mind, so put me there on time. Keep
You have bro - ken your vow and it's all o - ver now, so I'm
I'm through with you; too bad you are blue, so keep

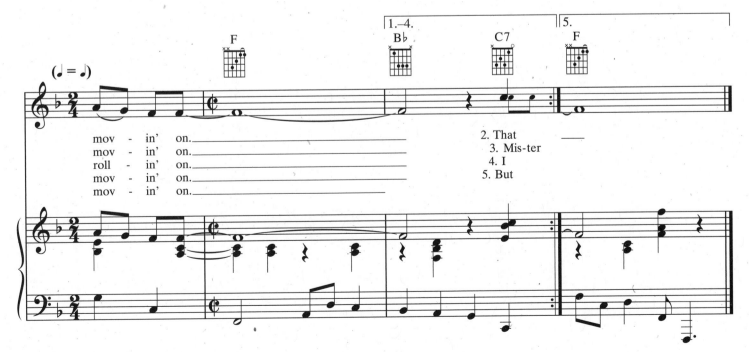

mov - in' on.
mov - in' on.
roll - in' on.
mov - in' on.
mov - in' on.

2. That
3. Mis - ter
4. I
5. But

I STILL MISS SOMEONE

Words and Music by
JOHNNY CASH and ROY CASH, JR.

JUST A LITTLE LOVIN'
(Will Go a Long Way)

Words and Music by
EDDIE ARNOLD and ZEKE CLEMENTS

Just a Little Lovin' - 3 - 1

NORTH TO ALASKA

Words and Music by
JOHNNY HORTON and
TILLMAN B. FRANKS

Moderate country two-beat ♩ = 84

North to A - las - ka,___ go north, the rush is on.___ 1. Big

Verses 1 & 2:

Sam left Se - at - tle in___ the year___ of nine - ty - two___ with

2. *See additional lyrics*

George___ Pratt, his part - ner, and broth - er Bill - y too.___ They

North to Alaska - 6 - 1

76

Where the

North to A - las - ka,___ go north,_

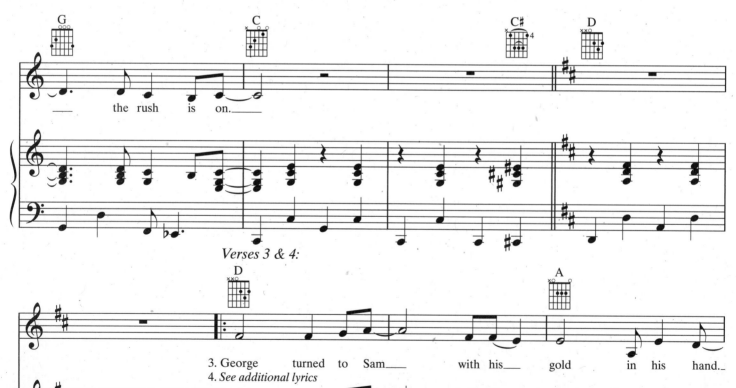

___ the rush is on.___

Verses 3 & 4:

3. George turned to Sam___ with his___ gold in his hand._
4. *See additional lyrics*

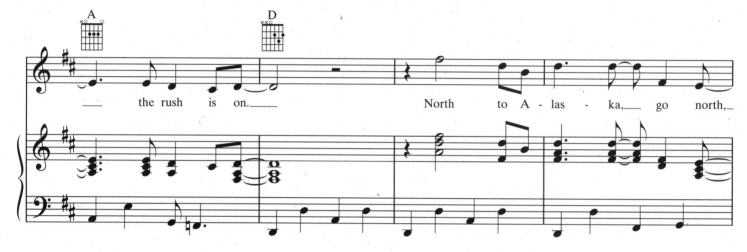

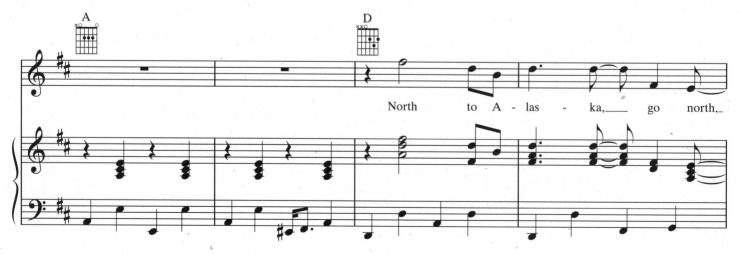

Verse 2:
Sam crossed the majestic mountains
To the valleys far below.
He talked to his team of huskies
As he mushed them through the snow,
With the northern lights runnin' wild
In the land of the midnight sun.
Yes, Sam McCord was a mighty man
In the year of nineteen-one.
(To Chorus:)

Verse 4:
'Cause a man needs a woman
To love him all the time.
You know Sam, a true love is hard to find.
I'd build for my Jenny a honeymoon home
Beneath that old white mountain,
Just a little southeast of Nome.
(To Chorus:)

PLEASE HELP ME, I'M FALLING

(In Love With You)

Words and Music by
HAL BLAIR and DON ROBERTSON

Moderate country two-beat

Please help me, I'm   fall - ing
oth - er
fall - ing

— in   love   with   you.   Close the door to temp -
whose   arms   have grown   cold.   But I prom-ised for -
and   that   would be   sin.   Close the door to temp -

Please Help Me, I'm Falling - 2 - 1

RIBBON OF DARKNESS

Words and Music by
GORDON LIGHTFOOT

Moderately fast ♩ = 108

Verses 1 & 2:

1. Rib - bon of dark -
2. Clouds are gath -

ness o - ver me._____ (whistling)

ness o - ver

LOVESICK BLUES

Words and Music by
IRVING MILLS and CLIFF FRIEND

SIXTEEN TONS

Words and Music by
MERLE TRAVIS

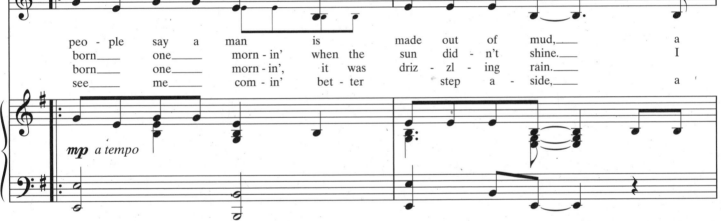

Sixteen Tons - 3 - 1

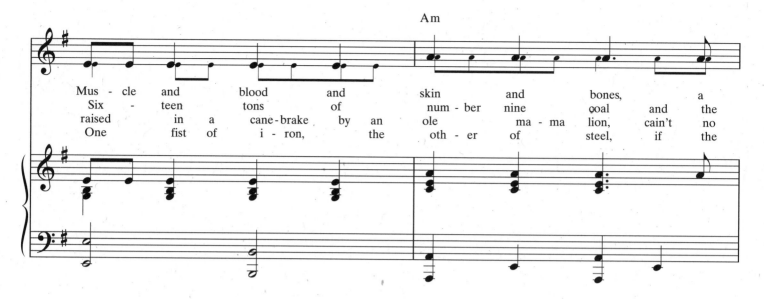

Mus - cle and blood and skin and bones, a
Six - teen tons of num - ber nine coal and a the
raised in a cane-brake by an ole ma - ma lion, cain't no
One fist of i - ron, the oth - er of steel, if the

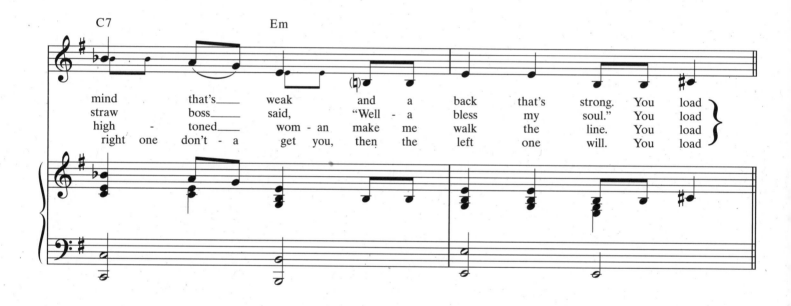

mind that's__ weak and a back that's strong. You load
straw boss__ said, "Well - a bless my soul." You load
high - toned__ wom - an make me walk the line. You load
right one don't - a get you, then the left one will. You load

Chorus:

Six - teen Tons, what do you get?__ An - oth - er day old - er and

SHAME ON YOU

Words and Music by
SPADE COOLEY

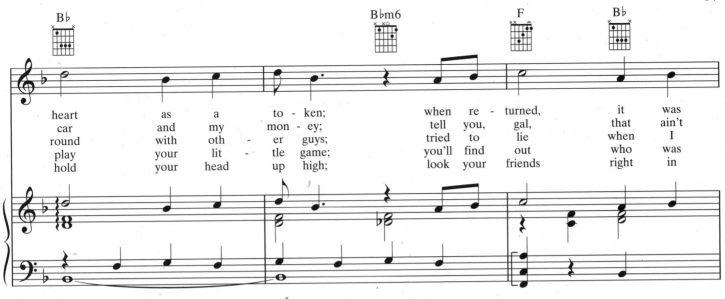

heart ... as a to-ken; ... when re-turned, ... it was
car ... and my mon-ey; ... tell you, gal, ... that ain't
round ... with oth-er guys; ... tried to lie ... when I
play ... your lit-tle game; ... you'll find out ... who was
hold ... your head up high; ... look your friends ... right in

bro-ken. Hide your face;_____ shame on
fun-ny. Durn your hide;_____ shame on
got wise. Fool-ish girl;_____ shame on
to blame. Hide your face;_____ shame on
the eye? No, you can't;_____ shame on

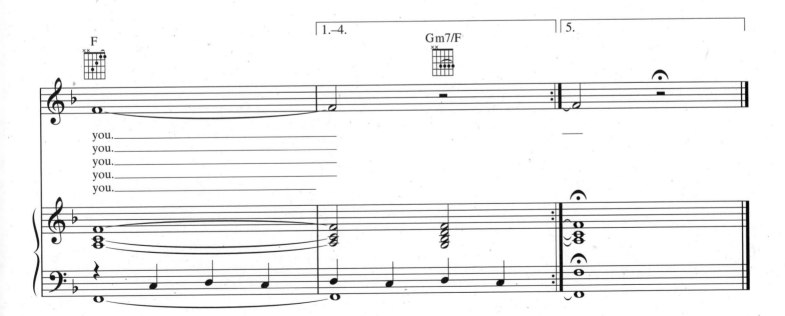

you._____
you._____
you._____
you._____
you._____

SMOKE! SMOKE! SMOKE!

(That Cigarette)

Words and Music by
MERLE TRAVIS and TEX WILLIAMS

STAND BY YOUR MAN

Words and Music by
TAMMY WYNETTE and BILLY SHERRILL

Some-times it's hard to be a wom-an,

giv-ing all you love to just one man.

Stand By Your Man - 5 - 1

WALKING THE FLOOR OVER YOU

Words and Music by
ERNEST TUBB

1. You left me and you went a - way.
(2.) dar - ling, you know I love you well,
(3.) some - day, you may be lone - some too.

You said that you'd be back in just a day.
love you more than I can ev - er tell.
Walk - ing the floor is good for you.

Walking the Floor Over You - 3 - 1

Chorus:

WINGS OF A DOVE

Words and Music by
BOB FERGUSON

Moderately bright

He sends down His love_____
He sent him His love_____
He sent Him His

on the wings of a dove._____

Chorus:

On the wings of a snow - white

dove, he sends his pure, sweet

THE YEAR THAT CLAYTON DELANEY DIED

Words and Music by
TOM T. HALL

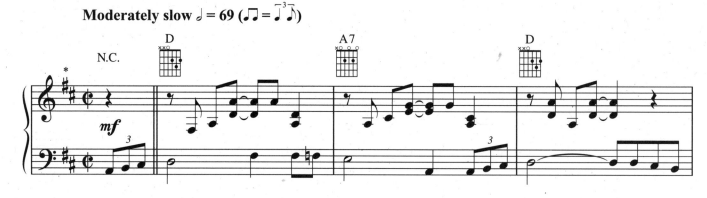

*Original recording in C# major.

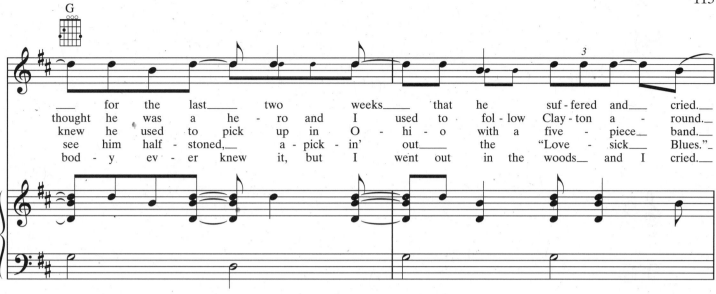

_for the last___ two weeks___ that he suf-fered and___ cried.___
thought he was a he-ro and I used to fol-low Clay-ton a-round.___
knew he used to pick up in O-hi-o with a five-piece___ band.___
see him half-stoned,___ a pick-in' out___ the "Love-sick___ Blues."___
bod-y ev-er knew it, but I went out in the woods and I cried.___

_ me,
_
_
_ It made___ a big im-pres-sion on___
I of-ten won-dered why Clay-
Clay-ton used to tell me,
When Clay-ton died, I made a prom-
Well, I know there's a lot of big preach-

_ me, al-though I was a bare-foot kid.___ They
ton, who seemed so good___ to me,___ I'd
ise: I was gon-na car-ry on___ some-how.___ There
ers that know a lot more than___ I do,___ but

said he got___ re - li - gion at the end, and I'm glad___ that he did.___
nev - er took___ his gui - tar and made it down in Ten - nes - see.___
ain't no mon - ey in it; it - 'll put you in an ear - ly grave."___
give a hun - dred dol - lars if he could on - ly see___ me now.___
it could be that the good Lord likes a lit - tle pick - in' too.___

1.–4.   5.

Yeah, I re -

3. Well,
4. I
5. I re -

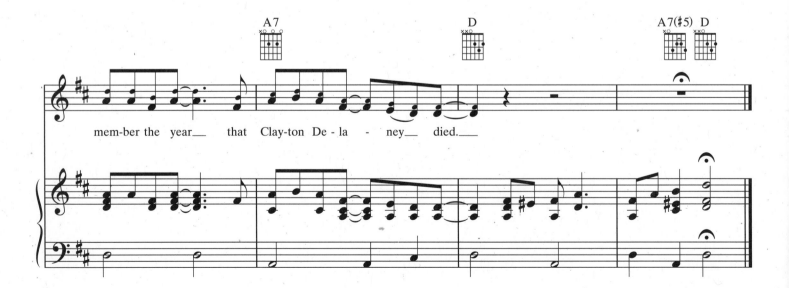

A7   D   A7(♯5) D

mem - ber the year___ that Clay-ton De - la - ney___ died.___

YOU DON'T KNOW ME

Words and Music by
CINDY WALKER
and EDDY ARNOLD

You give your hand to me_____ and___ then you say hel-lo._____ I can hard-ly speak,___ my___ heart is beat-ing so._____ And an-y-one could tell_____ you think you know me well,_____ but___ you don't know me._____ No,___ you don't know the one_____ who dreams of you at night___ and longs to

BRINGING YOU OVER 48,000 TITLES OF TODAY'S HITS AND YESTERDAY'S CLASSICS!

Working on a Dream
Bruce Springsteen
(00-32204)
Book, $19.95

Greatest Hits
Bruce Springsteen
(00-PF9541)
Book, $19.95

Mothership
Led Zeppelin
(00-30381)
Book, $24.95

Dream Theater Keyboard Experience
Dream Theater featuring Jordan Rudess
(00-32032)
Book, $26.95

The Van Halen Keyboard Songbook
Van Halen
(00-27506)
Book, $14.95

In Rainbows
Radiohead
(00-29220)
Book, $19.95

One of the Boys
Katy Perry
(00-31810)
Book, $16.95

Wincing the Night Away
The Shins
(00-28009)
Book, $19.95

American Idiot
Green Day
(00-PFM0506)
Book, $19.95

The Open Door
Evanescence
(00-27640)
Book, $19.95

Vampire Weekend
Vampire Weekend
(00-30733)
Book, $19.95

The Lost Christmas Eve
Trans-Siberian Orchestra
(00-30552) Book, $21.95

SELECTIONS FROM TODAY'S BOX OFFICE HITS

Harry Potter Musical Magic: The First Five Years
Music from Motion Pictures 1-5
(00-32033)
Book, $19.95

The Lord of the Rings: The Fellowship of the Ring
Music by Howard Shore
(00-0659B)
Book, $14.95

Corpse Bride: Selections from the Motion Picture
Music by Danny Elfman
(00-27925)
Book, $16.95

Star Wars: A Musical Journey (Music from Episodes I – VI)
Music by John Williams
(00-28303)
Book, $19.95

The Dark Knight: Selections from the Motion Picture
(00-31866)
Book, $14.95

Indiana Jones and the Kingdom of the Crystal Skull: Selections from the Motion Picture
Music by John Williams
(00-31379)
Book, $12.95

AVAILABLE at YOUR FAVORITE MUSIC RETAILER

Alfred Music Publishing
LEARN · TEACH · PLAY